Kids'
BOOK OF
GROSS
FACTS
&
FEATS

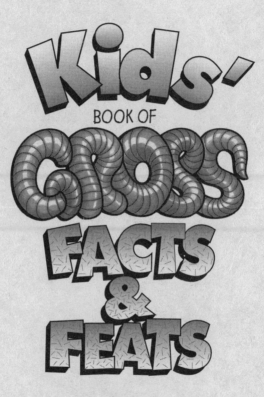

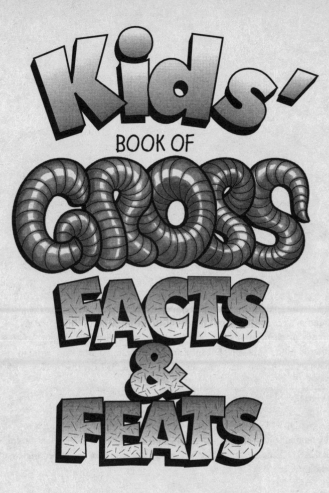

Kids'
BOOK OF
GROSS FACTS & FEATS

by Todd Strasser

illustrated by Donna Reynolds

SCHOLASTIC INC.

New York   Toronto   London   Auckland   Sydney
Mexico City   New Delhi   Hong Kong   Buenos Aires

ISBN 0-439-65349-5

12 11 10 9 8 7 6 5   5 6 7 8 9/0

Printed in the U.S.A.   40

First Scholastic printing, January 2004

To Ship, Debbie, Rachel, and Daniel Green—
good, not gross, people.

The Grossest Part of Your Body

People may have told you that you had a gross mouth.

Or a disgusting mouth.

Or something like that.

They were right—but for the wrong reason.

They may have been referring to something you *said*.

But it's what's *in* your mouth that's really gross.

That's because more than 300 different kinds of creatures live in your mouth!

The Grossest Part of Your Body

Continued

Most of the creatures living in your mouth are microorganisms. I said *most* because maybe you're that one person in a million who keeps a pet tadpole in his mouth.

Microorganisms are really small, which is a good thing because around 150,000,000 of them live in your mouth at any given time.

That's right, 150,000,000, or roughly 500,000 of each of the 300 different types.

Here's another way to look at it: If each of those microorganisms was a human being, more than half the entire population of the United States would live in your mouth!

(That's a Big Mouth.)

And Speaking of Big Mouths

When a bullfrog gets hungry, there's no telling what it will eat.

And that includes other bullfrogs.

Bullfrogs don't take little bites.

They just eat each other whole.

(Can I have one with green slime sauce?)

The Gross Olympics

Spitting:

Gold

The world's record for spitting a cherry pit is 95 feet (29 meters).

Silver

The world's record for spitting a watermelon seed is 75 feet (23 meters).

Bronze

The world's record for spitting tobacco juice is 49 feet (15 meters).

More Gross Olympics

Eating Weird Stuff:

Gold

The gold medal goes to a man from Grenoble, France, who takes the cake (ha!) for eating the weirdest stuff. Since 1959 he has been eating roughly (believe it!) 2 pounds (.9 kilogram) of metal and glass a day.

Here's some of the stuff he's eaten:

A Cessna airplane (I'll have my wings with hot sauce!)

A computer (Love those chips!)

A TV set

(These aren't all the strange things he's eaten. Turn the page and keep reading . . .)

A bicycle (Even the seat! Yuck!)

A coffin (Thus making him the only person in history to put a coffin in a man rather than a man in a coffin!)

Eating Weird Stuff,

Continued

Silver

The silver medal goes to a Chinese man who eats live animals. In one recent year he ate two ducks, six chickens, twenty-five frogs, twenty lizards, and fifteen rats.

The man has also eaten four poisonous snakes, plant roots, and uncooked pork.

Eating Weird Stuff,

Continued Again

"Lead"

A lead medal goes to the Australian electrician who was diagnosed with lead poisoning after eating about 3 feet (91 centimeters) of electrical cable a day. The man claimed the cable had a "sweet and pleasant taste, especially near the center."

He was hospitalized after complaining of abdominal pain and constipation.

Still Eating Weird Stuff

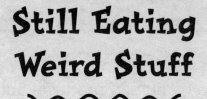

Bronze

The bronze medal goes to the man who bit off Scott Irvine's nose in a fight. Mr. Irvine showed up at the hospital with his nose, and doctors tried to reattach it. At the time of the report, they were not sure the operation was a success.

• • •

Dishonorable mention to heavyweight boxer Mike Tyson, who was disqualified when he bit off part of defending champ Evander Holyfield's ear in a title fight.

More on Spitting

The average human produces about a quart of saliva every day.

That's about 6,000 gallons (22,710 liters) in a lifetime and just enough to fill a small swimming pool.

(Hey, want to come over for a swim?

Gee, the water looks a little weird.)

Speaking of Spit
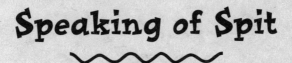

You may have heard that when angered, both llamas and camels will spit at their adversaries.

One scientist decided to measure how much spit a camel produces.

He discovered that the average camel spitball weighs 200 grams (almost half a pound!). Most of it is comprised of disgusting camel phlegm.

(Duck!)

Gross Stupidity

A thief in Bangkok, Thailand, stole a woman's purse and then ran into a building he thought was a Buddhist temple. Unfortunately for him, it was a police station. The thief hid in a bathroom until the police noticed something weird.

They arrested him.

Gross Stupidity,

Continued

A man in Redondo Beach, California, was arrested for drunk driving after police saw him driving down the highway with half a traffic-light pole, including the lights, lying across the hood of his car.

When questioned, the man said he thought the lights "came with the car" when he bought it.

Gross Stupidity,

Further Continued

A woman robber held up several people in a shoe store and took their wallets. When a police officer began to chase the thief, she dropped the wallets in a garbage can.

One of the wallets she dropped was her own.

An officer arrested her the next day when she called the police station to report that her wallet was missing.

Gross Breath

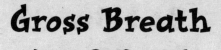

Most of the 150,000,000 microorganisms found in your mouth are bacteria, which are what some people call germs.

Most of those bacteria won't hurt you, but they are living things—like you and me. And like you and me, they eat stuff and excrete waste.

Ever notice that the longer you go without brushing your teeth, the worse your breath smells?

Guess what's causing your bad breath?

Bacteria excretions.

(Smile.)

Bad Breath in Houses

Our mouths may be filled with bacteria, but our houses and apartments are filled with mold.

Have you sneezed lately? You might be allergic to mold spores, which molds release in order to reproduce.

Do you have asthma or sinus problems? Mold causes those too. In fact, some varieties of mold can cause flu-like symptoms, including coughing, a runny nose, and a burning throat.

So just where is the mold in your house? Everywhere.

All mold needs is water and something yummy to munch on. Ever catch a whiff of mildew in the basement? That's mold.

Ever find fuzzy bluish-gray spots on bread or cheese? Mold again.

And mold just loves damp wallpaper in the bathroom.

Guess what that dark brown or black stuff along the edge of the bathtub and behind the sink is?

(Feel like moving yet?)

Gross on Ice

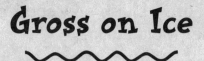

In Jerusalem, police tried to get a man to take his dead seventy-year-old mother out of his refrigerator. He was keeping her there until science could bring her back to life.

"It's very hard for me," the man explained. "But this was her wish."

(Hope he has his eyes wide open when he goes for a midnight snack.)

Gross on Ice,

Continued

Armed with an arrest warrant, federal agents went to the home of a man in Charlottesville, Virginia, who was suspected of possessing illegal drugs.

The man was supposed to be home, but they'd couldn't find him until they opened his refrigerator.

He was hiding inside, drinking a soda.

Toe Cheese

Toe cheese is the mushy stuff that collects between your toes and under your toenails.

It's called toe *cheese* because, just like some cheeses, it smells.

Toe cheese is made up of lots of stuff:

Sock fibers

Dead skin

Sweat

Fungus

Bacteria (our good buddies)

The Speed of Grossness

Sneezes leave your mouth and nose traveling at more than 100 miles (161 kilometers) per hour.

(Gentlemen, start your noses!)

Winds on the planet Saturn sometimes exceed 1,000 miles (1,609 kilometers) per hour.

(Okay, so it's not gross, but it is amazing!)

The Speed of More Grossness

Everyone knows that the cheetah is the fastest land animal. It can run 60 miles (97 kilometers) per hour.

But that's only for a short distance—up to 600 yards (548 meters).

One of the fastest long-distance land runners is a . . . bird!

(Wait a minute! You said *land* animal!)

That's right. One of the fastest land animals for long distances is the ostrich, which can travel a long way at up to 40 miles (64 kilometers) per hour and cover more than 25 feet (8 meters) with each step.

The ostrich can't fly, so it's considered a land animal.

(Okay, that fact about ostriches isn't gross. But read the next page.)

Speaking of Ostriches

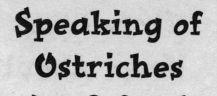

People in the desert used to think that ostriches stuck their heads in the sand when they were scared.

They did stick their heads in the sand but not because they were scared.

They did it because they were hungry!

Ostriches eat sand!

It helps them digest other food.

More Gross News About Microorganisms

~~~~~~~~~

Just like us, bacteria need moisture.

Think of some of the smelly parts of your body. Your mouth, your armpits, your feet.

What do those smelly parts all have in common? Moisture.

Foot sweat and bacteria—it's a marriage made in smell heaven.

• • •

Here's another fact guaranteed to totally gross you out. If your body was freeze dried, 10 percent of your body weight would be from the microorganisms living in there right now!

Even More Gross News About Microorganisms

By the way, you may have noticed fungus back there on the toe-cheese page.

Fungi can be microscopic organisms like bacteria. But unlike bacteria, they can also grow pretty big. Mushrooms are a type of fungi and, therefore, are related to the fungi in toe cheese.

Think about that the next time you order a pizza with mushrooms.

Most types of fungi like to eat decaying plant or animal matter. The typical fungi in toe cheese eat dead skin cells.

Some other types of fungi aren't so particular. They don't mind eating living cells too. If you've ever had athlete's foot or ringworm, you know what I'm talking about.

By the way, ringworm isn't a worm, it's a fungus.

The Grossest Creatures in Your Lawn

When it comes to gross animals, worms are major contenders for the most-gross-and-disgusting award.

You know worms—those slimy, creepy crawly things that slither around in the earth and come out after it rains.

Did you know that there are 2,700 different kinds of earthworms alone?

Worms,

Continued

~~~~~~~~

Worms aren't always small. The Australian giant Gippsland earthworm grows up to 6 feet (2 meters) in length and weighs up to 1½ pounds (.7 kilogram).

(Yummy when boiled and served on a bed of mud!)

The largest earthworm ever found was discovered in South Africa. It was 22 feet (7 meters) long.

(Enough to feed a whole family!)

Worms,

Continued Again

Each worm is both male and female. (Which means they always have a date on Saturday night!)

A typical acre of farmland generally contains several *million* worms.

More Gross Stupidity

Two Arkansas men were driving home after a night of frog hunting when the lights on their pickup truck went out. After inspecting the truck, they decided that the headlight fuse had burned out.

They didn't have an extra fuse, but one of the men noticed that the fuse was about the same size as a .22-caliber bullet. He had plenty of those and stuck a bullet where the fuse was supposed to go.

About half an hour later the overheated bullet went off, striking the driver in the leg. The truck veered off the road and smashed into a tree.

When the injured man's wife heard what happened, she asked if, after all that trouble, they'd managed to find any frogs.

More Gross Stupidity,

Continued

A man in Sandusky, Ohio, was charged with negligent assault after he fired his shotgun at what he thought was a rat.

The "rat" turned out to be his wife's hat, which she was wearing at the time.

The man had previously shot himself in the leg while trying to hit a rat.

(Talk about bad aim!)

More Gross Stupidity,

Continued Further

A Kansas man was charged with holding up a shoe store and stealing about $70 cash and a pair of tan hiking boots.

The man showed up for his trial wearing the tan hiking boots.

The man was found guilty. The boots were returned to the shoe store.

Gross Danger

One of the most poisonous creatures on earth is a frog.

The poison-arrow frog carries enough poison to kill more than 2,000 people.

South American natives use the poison on arrows to hunt animals. The poison paralyzes the animal when it gets into its bloodstream.

More Gross Danger

A medical researcher in South Africa "milked" more than half a million poisonous snakes over a ten-year period.

Without being bitten once!

His work produced almost 900 gallons (3,407 liters) of snake venom, which is used to heal snake-bite victims.

Even More
Gross Danger

~~~~~~

- The ostrich can kill a man by . . . kicking him in the head.

- The spitting cobra overcomes its enemies by . . . spitting venom into their eyes.

- When attacked, the common slug fights back by . . . releasing a third of its weight in mucus! (Think it's related to the camel?)

- The Mexican elephant tree protects its leaves from being eaten by . . . squirting oil.

- The horned toad (actually a lizard) fends off attackers by . . . squirting blood from its eyes.

Gross-Insect Test

Name this insect:

It has white blood and at least eighteen knees.

Its kidneys look like a bunch of writhing snakes.

It can live for a week without its head.

There are more than 5,000 different species of this insect worldwide.

Some people in South America eat them as snacks.

Answer: cockroach

More Gross Insect Facts

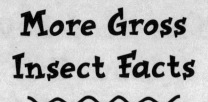

After eating, a house fly regurgitates its food and eats it again.

(Man, that was so good, I ate it twice!)

(Guess if you're a fly, you always have seconds!)

Also, if a soldier in the Civil War developed an infection from a wound, fly maggots were sometimes put on the wound to eat the pus.

(Yum!)

The Good News About Pus

~~~~~~~~

You know what pus is. It's the whitish stuff that oozes out of a cut that has become infected.

It's also the white stuff inside pimples that sort of make your face look like pizza pie when you have a bad case of acne.

Believe it or not, pus is actually good stuff. It means that the good guys in your body (white blood cells) are fighting the bad guys (often bacteria).

(Oh, no! Not bacteria again! Those critters are everywhere!)

What Pus Boils Down To

Boils are the "blue whales" of the pimple world. They're like pimples—only bigger, and deeper under your skin.

Sometimes they really hurt.

Sometimes a doctor will lance a boil. That means he'll cut it open with a really sharp, sterile scalpel (knife).

Then the doctor can remove the pus.

(I wonder if Sir Lance-a-Lot was really a doctor?)

Gross Food from Around the World

Mexico: lamb-brain tacos

Japan: broiled beetle grubs

China: sun-dried maggots

Samoa: baked bat

The Most Unlikely Fact

Question:

Ever smell a skunk? It really stinks.

So guess what that disgusting liquid skunk spray is used for?

Answer: A perfume ingredient.

(Who're you calling stinky?)

Gross Plumbing

People used to tell stories about giant alligators living in the sewers.

The alligators supposedly got there because they were bought as pets when they were babies.

Later, when they grew too big or bit off someone's finger, the owners would just flush them down the toilet.

It turns out that someone in Arizona actually did this with a boa constrictor.

No one knows how long the boa constrictor lived in the sewers.

But one day it came up through a toilet and scared a woman who couldn't understand why her toilet was clogged.

Gross Logic

An inmate who escaped from a Tennessee jail stole a car and led police on a chase sometimes reaching 150 miles (241 kilometers) per hour. After he was captured, the inmate explained that he had always intended to turn himself in.

He said he was driving fast because he "wanted to get far enough ahead" of the police to make it clear that he was giving up on his own.

Gross Logic,

Continued

A drunk German man went to see his girlfriend, but she wouldn't talk to him because he'd been drinking.

The man decided he could get the woman to talk to him if he rammed her house with a four-and-a-half-ton construction excavator.

The woman still wouldn't talk to him. But the police did. They arrested him.

Tapeworms

Tapeworms like to live in the intestines of other animals. There they eat the partially digested food the animal has consumed.

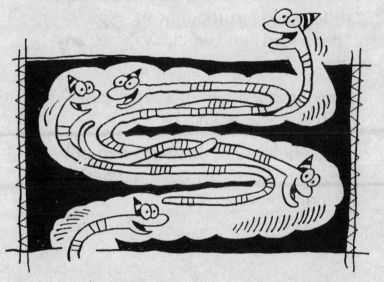

It's a good life, because all the tapeworms have to do is hang out and wait for the food to come to them.

Some tapeworms grow to be 60 feet (18 meters) long. Sometimes they live in human intestines!

Gross Roommates

A woman and her son lived with the woman's dead mother for several months.

They reportedly didn't believe she was dead. They just thought she was "depressed" and would wake up any time.

They propped her up in front of a TV set with her eyes open.

Police noted that the woman didn't hesitate to cash her dead mother's social security checks.

Gross History

One early type of human being, *Homo sapiens neanderthalensis,* otherwise known as Neanderthal man, used to eat his enemies' brains.

(Guess he thought he'd get smarter that way!)

Gross History,

Continued

The Massagetae, an ancient tribe, didn't wait for their elders to die. When they got old enough, they were killed, boiled, and eaten.

(At least the Massagetae never went hungry.)

• • •

The Chavins, a tribe in Peru, smoked dead bodies over a fire—much the way meats and fish are smoked today.

Gross History,

Continued Again

The Aztecs used to sacrifice about 250,000 of their own people each year, usually by cutting their hearts out while they were still alive.

Supposedly, they did it because they believed an evil sun god would destroy them if they didn't feed him a special kind of honey that they thought came only from human hearts.

("Have a heart!"

"Thanks. Uh, could you pass the mustard?")

Gross Munitions

A man in Sarajevo, Bosnia, reportedly got mad at his wife . . . and tried to shoot her with a bazooka.

The woman fled from the house, and the man followed. He fired the bazooka.

It missed the woman and hit their house.

"It caused serious damage," said a United Nations spokesman.

(Bet it didn't do much for their relationship either!)

Gross Animal Stuff

- Elephants have been known to remain standing after they die. Elephants also have the largest teeth (their tusks) of all living animals.

- During digestion, cows produce large amounts of methane gas (so do humans). Methane gas is extremely flammable. Cows have been known to spontaneously combust (nah, just kidding!).

- Sharks can get a sunburn if they float on the surface for too long. However, they cannot develop melanoma, a cancerous condition humans can get from too much sun.

- One of the ingredients in lipstick is fish scales.

- Fish have been known to produce offspring with five heads on one body. (Pentaguppy!)

Speaking of Weird Fish

A certain type of fish that lives near Japan can be a boy or a girl. If it starts out as a boy, it finds a couple of girl fish and hangs around them.

However, if a bigger boy fish comes along, the smaller boy fish will turn itself into a *girl* fish!

And if the bigger boy fish gets bored and leaves, the smaller boy fish, who turned itself into a girl fish, can turn itself back into a boy fish!

(Can we get that fish on *Oprah*?)

More Gross Animal Stuff

~~~~~~~~~

- The heart of a giraffe is 2 feet (61 centimeters) long and weighs 25 pounds (11 kilograms).

- An octopus has three hearts. (It could become the world's only living heart donor.)

- If human babies grew as fast as a baby blue whale, a human would be 65 feet (20 meters) tall by the time he was two years old. By the way, an adult blue whale's heart weighs half a ton (.45 metric ton) and generates 10 horsepower to pump the 8 tons (7 metric tons) of blood in its body.

- The embryos of tiger sharks fight to the death while still in the mother's womb. Only the survivor is born.

Even More Gross Animal Stuff

- The giraffe's tongue is nearly 2 feet (61 centimeters) long. It uses it . . . to clean out its ears!

- Slugs may be able to expel one third of their body weight in mucus, but the world champion mucus producer has to be the hagfish. The hagfish doesn't look much like a fish. It looks a lot more like a long, fat tube of slime. It has hundreds of tiny glands outside its body that continually produce mucus. (I usually keep the fish I catch, but I think I'll let this one go.)

And Speaking of Gross Animal Stuff

A lamb born in Spain had a fifth leg growing out of its head.

The leg was perfectly formed and was surgically removed.

Before the operation, the lamb's owner reported that the five-legged lamb was much livelier than his other sheep.

(I'll have a leg of lamb, please!)

Gross Insect and Spider Stuff

- The male of one species of insect related to the praying mantis can reproduce only after the female has bitten off its head.

- A mosquito has forty-seven teeth.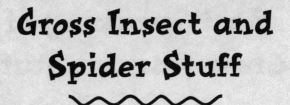

- Mosquitos have killed more people (by spreading disease) than all the world's wars.

- The total weight of all the insects on earth is twelve times the total weight of all the people.

- In any given acre of green land you can expect to find about 50,000 spiders.

- A spider's blood is clear.

Gross Insubordination

Prison inmates may be in jail, but that just gives some of them time to think up ridiculous lawsuits against their prisons. For example:

- One inmate in New York sued the state for $10 million after he was charged with leaving a work-release job and trying to escape. The inmate claimed that "poor medical care" caused him to have amnesia and that he "forgot" to return to prison.

- Another inmate sued because he claimed that secondhand smoke was causing him to have medical problems. One big problem was that the inmate himself was a smoker.

Gross Weirdness

When pulled over for driving without his seat belt, a man in Los Angeles told a police officer he'd done it because he wanted to smell his feet.

Gross Weirdness,

Continued

A man in Arhus, Denmark, was discovered walking naked through the streets in sub-zero temperatures.

Police reported he was sleepwalking.

Gross Justice

- In the Middle Ages the highest court in France ordered the execution of a cow for injuring a man.

- Recently a homeless man in Florida faced a mandatory jail sentence of forty years for stealing twenty-two rolls of toilet paper with a value of less than $15.

- In New York, a dog was ordered by a judge to see a psychiatrist for biting the nose of a two-year-old girl.

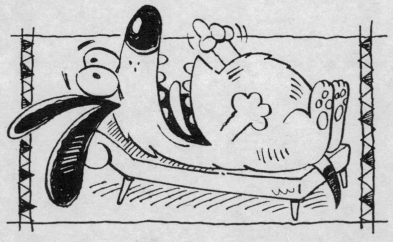

More Gross Justice

~~~~~~~~~~

A forty-eight-year-old Cincinnati, Ohio, man—who is blind—was given a ticket for jaywalking after he was hit by a pickup truck.

The man suffered broken bones.

Cincinnati prosecutors eventually dropped the jaywalking charge.

Gross Injustice

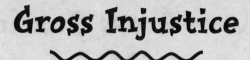

- In Hamburg, Germany, a pet kangaroo was thrown in jail after it escaped from its owner.

- In Jakarta, Indonesia, police in the town of Bekasi have asked permission to use poisonous cobras to force suspects into confessing to crimes. They are also considering using them as "riot-control weapons." (Stop laughing or I'll sick my cobra on you.)

Gross Injustice,

Continued

~~~~~~

A thirteen-year-old Oregon boy got in trouble for breaking his school's zero-tolerance-to-alcohol policy.

The beverage in question was a bottle of Scope mouthwash.

The boy explained that he wanted to rinse his mouth because "lunch tasted kind of bad."

He was suspended for a week.

Maladjusted Justice

A Sydney, Australia, man was convicted of assault on a police officer who pulled him over for a traffic violation.

The driver was accused of intentionally chewing on garlic before breathing into the police officer's face.

Gross Miscalculation

~~~~~~

Two armed robbers in Ontario, Canada, thought it would be easy to hold up a grocery store run by a seventy-five-year-old woman.

They were wrong. During the robbery attempt, she smashed one of them on the head with a large can of tomatoes.

The men ran away.

"I work hard for my money," the elderly lady said. "No one's going to take it away from me."

Gross Bedmates

The average bedroom mattress contains 6,000,000 dust mites.

You can't see them, and they don't bite.

Bedbugs, however, are visible to the naked eye—and they do bite.

Bedbugs are tiny six-legged creatures that like to come out at night and drink blood.

With the aid of powerful muscles in their heads, they are able to suck blood out of sleeping people.

More Gross Food from Around the World

~~~

Norway: beef blood pudding

Tanzania: white-ant pie

Peru: barbecued cow heart

Indonesia: coconut-cream marinated dog

Laos: roasted caterpillars

Mexico: honeyed ants

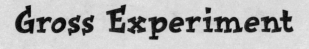

Gross Experiment

A nine-year-old boy in Glenwood Springs, Colorado, decided to see if it's really true that your tongue will stick to frozen metal.

The boy pressed his tongue against a streetlight pole.

He had to get help from the fire department to free his tongue.

"It stuck," the boy concluded.

Gross Ineptitude

A Danish burglar was locked in jail, but that didn't stop him from pursuing his career.

At night he would push apart the bars in his cell and sneak out.

Police became suspicious when they discovered roughly $6,000 worth of stolen merchandise in his cell.

Gross Science Mistakes

Early scientists attempted to identify prehistoric animals based on the bones they found. But sometimes they made mistakes.

Reconstructed skeletons of the elephant and its predecessor, the mammoth, were occasionally given antlers.

Other scientists assumed that the elephant was the mythical one-eyed cyclops. They decided this after noticing that elephant skulls had a large hole in the middle. They thought it was the eye socket.

Actually, it was the nasal passage connecting the elephant's trunk to its lungs.

More Gross Science Mistakes

~~~~~~

The science of studying old bones is called paleontology, and those who practice it are called paleontologists.

One of the first paleontologists was Sir Richard Owen, who supervised the reconstruction of a large dinosaur called the *Iguanodon.*

When Sir Richard finished his project, he invited twenty important dignitaries to dine in the dinosaur's belly.

Today scientists know that Sir Richard's reconstruction of the *Iguanodon* was fairly accurate—except for the horn of the dinosaur's snout, which turned out to be one of its toes.

(Give that dinosaur a nose job!)

More Gross History

In the 1700s wigs were fashionable for both men and women in France. But the wigs had to have slits in them. Why?

So that head lice and other insects could get out.

Of Bones and Barbarians

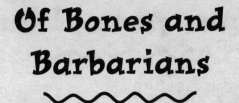

In the 1300s a Mongolian barbarian named Tamerlane liked to erect pyramids to himself using thousands of skulls from his victims.

Scottish barbarians also recycled skulls but preferred to wear the heads of their victims on their belts.

Gross Animal Quiz

Name this creature:

It lives in the wild; it is also raised by humans in freshwater farms; and it comes in more than 600 varieties up to 18 inches (46 centimeters) long.

It likes to suck blood. In a mere twenty minutes it can suck up to five times its own body weight in blood.

This species is so popular that it even has its own museum in Charleston, South Carolina.

It secretes an enzyme in its mouth that counteracts coagulation—which is the ability of blood to clot so that we don't bleed to death. By stopping coagulation, this creature ensures it will have a hearty meal of free-flowing blood.

In the 1800s doctors used it to treat obesity, insanity, insomnia, and migraine headaches (by letting it suck the blood from peoples' heads!).

It is used in medicine today by plastic surgeons, who take advantage of its anticoagulating enzymes during reconstructive surgery.

Answer: The leech.

Gross Irony

A man in Charlotte, North Carolina, held up a convenience store, using a rock as a weapon.

A bunch of teenagers hanging around outside the store saw the crime and chased the criminal.

They caught him, took his money, and left.

Gross Irony,

Continued

A robber trying to take a 600-pound (272-kilogram) safe down a flight of stairs was crushed to death when he lost his footing and fell.

The safe landed on top of him.

It was reported that the safe held no money.

It was filled with insurance forms.

(What that guy needed was an insurance *application!*)

Very Unsafe

Police in Sioux Falls, South Dakota, arrested two burglars for stealing a safe.

It was a large safe, and they were driving a small sports car.

They put the safe in the trunk.

Police pulled them over when they noticed a safe sticking out of the trunk.

Gross Irony,

Continued Again

A fire demolished an expensive vacation home owned by the president of a large cigarette company.

Firefighters speculated that the blaze was started by a construction worker who carelessly dropped . . . a cigarette!

Gross Customs

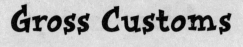

The members of a tribe in Africa spit at each other as a way to show respect.

In Tibet they just stick out their tongues at you.

Sounds crazy, right? But here's something really insane: In medieval times, if they thought you were crazy, they *drilled a hole in your head!*

Things were definitely strange back then. In fact, some medieval Europeans thought that brushing their teeth with urine would make them whiter. (They sure saved money on toothpaste!)

Gross Insensitivity

A kindergarten teacher in Charleston, South Carolina, was suspended for twenty days without pay for writing "Where are my glasses?" on a student's face.

The teacher was allowed back into the classroom on the condition that she enter a "sensitivity training" program.

Gross Accident

A nine-year-old girl was injured after being sucked into the toilet during a South African Airways flight.

A spokesman for the airline said nothing like that had ever happened before.

Gross Teacher Abuse

Two high-school girls decided to play a prank on their teachers by baking them chocolate brownies filled with a chocolate-flavored laxative.

They left the brownies in the teachers' lounge, where eight teachers ate them.

The girls were arrested and faced up to five years in jail.

(I'll be out in a minute!)

Even More Gross Stupidity

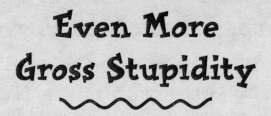

A burglar in New Jersey picked a lock on a door, but he needed something to place in the doorjamb so that it wouldn't lock again while he was inside.

The man reached into his pocket, took out a piece of paper, folded it several times, and stuck it between the door and the doorjamb.

He proceeded to rob the place, then left.

While investigating the burglary the next morning, a police officer found the paper and read it—it was a traffic ticket complete with the burglar's name and address.

The burglar was arrested.

Even More Gross Stupidity,

Continued

During a cold spell in Europe, a Belgian truck driver discovered that the fuel in his fuel tank had frozen.

He tried to melt the fuel with a blow torch.

Even More Gross Food from Around the World

China: fried grasshoppers

Philippines: pigs feet with bananas

Ghana: stewed cat

France: stuffed calf's eyes

United States: baked armadillo

• • •

Do you like Jell-O? Just about everybody does. The basic ingredient in Jell-O is gelatin, which is made from crushed animal bones. Yum!

Gross Incompetence

Bank employees in Tacoma, Washington, forgot that an eighty-six-year-old woman was inside a bank vault. She was checking her safe-deposit box when they closed up for the day. Not until the next morning did they reopen the vault and find her.

"It was dark in there," she told the police.

(Good thing it wasn't a weekend!)

And Finally, Crooks More Grossly Stupid Than You Can Imagine

A man was arrested for trying to steal a television from a K-Mart in Pennsylvania.

The judge released him on $2,500 bail.

He walked out of the courtroom and caught a cab to the same K-Mart, where he tried to steal the same TV again.

He was arrested again.

• • •

A bank robber in Baltimore was arrested when police found him standing outside the bank counting the money he'd just stolen.

About the Author

Todd Strasser has written many award-winning novels for young and teenage readers. His books published by Troll include *Hey, Dad, Get a Life!* and *The Kids' Book of Insults.* Among his other books are *Help! I'm Trapped in Obedience School* and *Girl Gives Birth to Own Prom Date.* He, his wife, and their children prefer not to think about bacteria.